WHO THIS BOOK IS FOR

This book approaches wedding reception planning from the perspective of a Master of Ceremonies (Emcee). From the moment a Bride & Groom become engaged, the planning process gets underway. This guide will provide you with insider information used by Bridal Consultants and Wedding Disc Jockeys & Emcees, to prepare the perfect wedding reception itinerary.

Well over a decade ago, I wrote an article, "21 Questions to Ask a DJ", and it has been published worldwide. While it still continues to be published online and in print in the most prestigious and well known bridal magazines, this book goes much further. It not only answers questions, but covers all aspects of planning your dream wedding reception. A sample legal contract addendum is also included, to ensure your wedding Disc Jockey & Emcee meets or surpasses professional standards.

While many books attempt to appeal to mass audiences, this one is written only for a select audience of three: For a Bride & Groom, for a Bridal Consultant/ Wedding Planner; and also for an Emcee (who may or may not be your Disc Jockey).

And it goes further than being a planning guide – it is also a tool you use to hire a professional Disc Jockey & Emcee. It contains ALL of the questions that you should be asking potential Disc Jockey companies, to ensure you get the right person for the job!

PREFACE:

Terry Dillon has been a professional wedding Disc Jockey and Emcee and owner of SoundsXtreme.com since 1997. He has written many full-length articles and had his work published world-wide in many prominent bridal magazines including Bliss Weddings and Brides. In addition, Terry is a professional course developer and writer, having been trained and employed by the Canadian government, Centre for Career Development (CCD). He has also been a feature column contributor for a national newspaper as well as having been published in other magazines and newspapers.

The Wedding Reception Entertainer Planner has been developed as a job aid to assist Bridal Consultants, Wedding Planners, Disc Jockeys and Masters of Ceremonies (Emcees), to prepare a wedding reception itinerary. Within these pages you will find a complete guide to planning all aspects of the wedding reception entertainment, and an additional tool to assist with ensuring professional Disc Jockey and Emcee standards.

As a special bonus, I've included a sample legal document we at SoundsXtreme.com provide to all of our wedding clients. This document is an ADDENDUM that contains ten "CertifyYourDJ.com" standards that may be printed out and included as an ADDENDUM to a LEGALLY BINDING WRITTEN CONTRACT between the Bride & Groom and their respective Disc Jockey & Emcee.

The document, "CertifyYourDJ.com Standards - ADDENDUM", has been ratified by:

Paul Sanderson
Sanderson Entertainment Law
577 Kingston Road, Suite 303
Toronto, Ontario, Canada
M4E 1R3
www.SandersonLaw.ca

Paul Sanderson has been exclusively serving clients in the entertainment industry for over 25 years. He is a lawyer, musician, poet and songwriter. For all your legal entertainment needs, we contact: PaulSanderson@SandersonLaw.ca

Should you wish a personalized planner, contact the author through the following website: **www.SoundsXtreme.com** or email: **DJ@SoundsXtreme.com**

Or mail: **Terry Dillon**
SoundsXtreme.com
919 Chipping Park Blvd.
Cobourg, Ontario K9A 5H2   Canada

Table of Contents

WEDDING RECEPTION ENTERTAINMENT PLANNER

BRIDE & GROOM CONTACT INFORMATION

Contact Us

Name:_____

Address:_____

_____

City:_____

Province/ State:_____ Postal/ Zip Code:_____

Evening/ weekend phone number:_____

Daytime phone number:_____

Best time to call:_____

Email address:_____

Preferred contact method:_____

Notes:_____

_____

_____

_____

_____

_____

WEDDING RECEPTION DATE

Date of reception:_____   Day of week:_____

Start time:_____   End time:_____

THE WEDDING PARTY

Bride/ Groom/ Spouse 1:_____

Bride/ Groom/ Spouse 2:_____

Introduce Bridal Couple As:_____

Best Man/ Person:_____

Bridesmaid 1:_____

Usher 1:_____

Bridesmaid 2:_____

Usher 2:_____

Bridesmaid 3:_____

Usher 3:_____

Bridesmaid 4:_____

Usher 4:_____

Flower Girl:_____

Ring Bearer:_____

Bride's Mother:_____

Bride's Father:_____

Groom's Mother:_____

Groom's Father:_____

Master of Ceremonies (Emcee):_____

Additional Emcee for Introductions:_____

Notes:
_____

_____

COCKTAIL MUSIC

Scheduled Start Time: _____

Genre and style
(e.g. Instrumental): _____

Particulars: : _____

DINNER MUSIC

Scheduled Start Time: _____

Genre and style
(e.g. Instrumental): _____

Particulars: : _____

SPECIAL DANCES

Approximate Start Time: _____

First Dance - Introduce Couple as: _____

First Dance Song: _____

Married couple ONLY for this dance? Yes: ☐ No: ☐

A second selection for PARENTS? Yes: ☐ No: ☐

Song title: _____

A selection for BRIDAL PARTY? Yes: ☐ No: ☐

Song title: _____

SNOWBALL Bridal Party dance? Yes: ☐ No: ☐

HEAD TABLE SPEECHES

Based on the distance from your Disc Jockey to the head table, which of the following would be most appropriate to use?

Wireless microphone? Yes ☐ No: ☐

Wired microphone? Yes ☐ No: ☐

P.A. system? Yes ☐ No: ☐

MEAL

Will there be a meal? Yes: ☐ No: ☐

If a meal, is it served or buffet? Served: ☐ Buffet: ☐

If a meal, when is it to be served? _____

WEDDING CAKE CUTTING

Will you be cutting the cake? Yes: ☐ No: ☐

If yes, when (it is customary after dinner)? _____

Will the cake be served? Yes: ☐ No: ☐

If yes, when (It is customary about 11PM)? _____

SWEETS AND COLD PLATE TABLE

Announce a Sweets or Cold Plate Table? Yes: ☐ No: ☐

If yes, when? (it is customary about 11PM, the same customary time to serve cake): _____

BOUQUET & GARTER TOSS

Will the Bride be throwing the bouquet?   Yes: ☐   No: ☐

If so, when? _____

Will the Groom be removing the garter?   Yes: ☐   No: ☐

Play "The Stripper" for garter removal?   Yes: ☐   No: ☐

Alternate music choice for garter removal: _____

SPECIAL ANNOUNCEMENTS

The Disc Jockey will be prepared to handle any special announcements that may be required during the evening. If there are any special guests from out-of-town, anniversaries or birthdays that you would like announced, please specify:

_____

_____

_____

_____

_____

BAR CLOSING

Is there a host or house bar?   Host: ☐   House: ☐

Announce last call for the bar?   Yes: ☐   No: ☐

Is there a venue policy for the 'last call' announcement?
(Customary 30 min. prior to reception end)

Notes: _____

_____

EVENT DETAILS

If you have attended events in the past with a Disc Jockey & Emcee, what did you like or dislike about the performances?

_____

_____

_____

Do you prefer a Disc Jockey that tries to BE the center of attention, or one that focuses the attention on the Bride & Groom? What separates a good Disc Jockey from a bad Disc Jockey?

_____

_____

_____

How YOU Envision Your Reception

THE *MOST* important question for the Bride and Groom: How do you envision YOUR Dream Wedding Reception?

_____

_____

_____

_____

_____

_____

_____

_____

_____

MUSIC PROGRAMMING

The following information is helpful in order for your Disc Jockey to put together the right music program for the evening:

Approximate total number of guests to attend:_____

Approximate number of guests between ages 5 - 18:_____

Approximate number of guests between ages 19 - 39:_____

Approximate number of guests between ages 40 - 59:_____

Approximate number of guests age 60+:_____

Do you have any 'music style' preferences
(e.g. country, rock, hip-hop, 50s-60s)?

_____

_____

MUSIC REQUESTS

As a general rule of thumb, Disc Jockeys accept song requests that are **recognizable**, **danceable** and **not likely to be offensive** to other guests in attendance. Based on their years of experience, your Disc Jockey will know which songs to play, and when it is appropriate to play them.

When a guest makes a song request, your Disc Jockey will consider several factors in deciding if and when it is appropriate to play. Your Disc Jockey will almost certainly reserve the right to program music based on their professional expertise. Song requests that do not meet your Disc Jockey's criteria are not likely to be played, **regardless** of who makes the request.

In addition to your Disc Jockey's judgment, the Bride & Groom may also have some specific selections they would not like played.

DO NOT PLAY

Are there any songs that should **NOT** be played? (e.g. Rump Shaker, I'm Too Sexy)?

_____   _____   _____

_____   _____   _____

_____   _____   _____

REQUESTS FOR SONGS ON THE DO NOT PLAY LIST

If '<u>Do not play</u>' songs are "requested"
would you like us to play them?   Yes: ☐   No: ☐

LAST DANCE

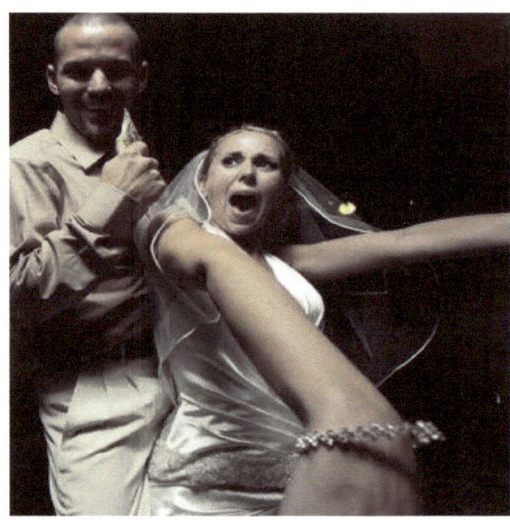

Typically, guests plan to leave the reception on the hour (often at midnight).   It is customary for the Bride & Groom to have their official 'Last Dance' prior to the departure of the majority of their guests.

Note, Brides & Grooms sometimes return to the reception to continue enjoying the party.

Last Dance Song: _____

Time for Last Song: _____

Notes: _____

_____

_____

_____

_____

_____

_____

_____

_____

_____

_____

CONTESTS, PARTY FAVOURS AND ENTERTAINERS

Zumba or ZumbAtomic? Yes: ☐ No: ☐ Maybe: ☐

Hawaiian Dancers/ Instruction? Yes: ☐ No: ☐ Maybe: ☐

Impersonators? Yes: ☐ No: ☐ Maybe: ☐

Comic or other Entertainer? Yes: ☐ No: ☐ Maybe: ☐

Interactive Dances? Yes: ☐ No: ☐ Maybe: ☐

Drinking Games? Yes: ☐ No: ☐ Maybe: ☐

Bride & Groom Slide Show (e.g. growing up)? Yes: ☐ No: ☐ Maybe: ☐

Party Favors or Glow Products? Yes: ☐ No: ☐ Maybe: ☐

Props such as hats, inflatable instruments? Yes: ☐ No: ☐ Maybe: ☐

Raffles or Door Prizes? Yes: ☐ No: ☐ Maybe: ☐

Lasers? Yes: ☐ No: ☐ Maybe: ☐

Mirror Ball? Yes: ☐ No: ☐ Maybe: ☐

Bubbles? Yes: ☐ No: ☐ Maybe: ☐

Strobe Light? Yes: ☐ No: ☐ Maybe: ☐

Notes: _____

_____

_____

_____

_____

_____

EVENT LOCATION (VENUE) DETAILS

Venue name: _____

Address: _____

_____

City: _____

Province/ State: _____ Zip/ Postal Code: _____

Contact Name: _____

Daytime phone number: _____

Best time to call: _____

Describe where the dance
floor is located, and where
the Disc Jockey is to setup: _____

_____

Building floor number: _____

Indoors or outdoors: _____

MUSIC FOR ADDITIONAL ROOMS

Is music required for additional rooms? (e.g. cocktails, wedding ceremony):

_____

_____

_____

_____

_____

_____

_____

ACCESSIBILITY: LOADING AND UNLOADING

What is the access from the loading zone to the designated Disc Jockey space?

Ground Level: ☐ Elevator: ☐

Loading ramp: ☐ Stairway: ☐

Number of stairs to move equipment: _____

Comments on accessibility: _____

At what time can your Disc Jockey enter and begin to set up? _____

At what time does the venue close? _____

At what time is your Disc Jockey required to be out of the venue? _____

Notes: _____

_____

_____

_____

_____

_____

_____

_____

_____

_____

_____

_____

_____

_____

_____

PLANNING FOR SUCCESS

RECEPTION BUDGET

What is the <u>total budget</u> for your reception?　　$ _____

IMPORTANCE OF ENTERTAINMENT

What PERCENTAGE does DANCING & ENTERTAINMENT make up, in the overall SUCCESS of your wedding reception?

25%	33%	40%	50%	66%	75%	80%	Higher

ENTERTAINMENT BUDGET

What percentage of your total reception budget is
allocated to the wedding Disc Jockey & Emcee?　　_____ %

What is the <u>dollar amount budgeted</u> to hiring the
wedding Disc Jockey & Emcee?　　$ _____

Notes: _____

_____

_____

_____

_____

_____

WEDDING DISC JOCKEY QUESTIONNAIRE

DISC JOCKEY COMPANY CONTACT INFORMATION

	Company #1	Company #2
Disc Jockey Company:		
Contact Name:		
Disc Jockey Performing:		
Company Address:		
Telephone Number:		
Cellular Number:		
Fax Number:		
Email Address:		
Website:		
Business Hours of Operation:		

Notes:

_____

_____

_____

_____

_____

_____

16 QUESTIONS TO ASK DISC JOCKEY COMPANIES

		Company #1	Company #2
1.	Will you personally be the Disc Jockey & Emcee for the wedding reception?		
2.	If not, can I meet the Disc Jockey & Emcee prior to signing a contract?		
3.	Do you also provide Emcee services for the reception?		
4.	Can you describe your training and experience as a wedding Disc Jockey & Emcee?		
5.	Do you come to my home or business to review the entertainment planner?		
6.	Do you completely setup and complete the testing of your equipment at least 30 minutes prior to guest arrival?		
7.	Do you wear a tuxedo or suit and tie as we request?		
8.	Do you offer lighting and sound upgrades?		
9.	What methods of payment do you accept?		
10.	How much is your non-refundable retainer, to begin work on planning our event and to reserve our date?		
11.	When is the non-refundable retainer due?		
12.	When is the final payment due and what method?		
13.	If you offer overtime, what is the rate?		
14.	Are there any additional charges not mentioned? (e.g. travel)		
15.	Do you provide a written contract and guarantee?		
16.	What are the cancellation terms?		

DISC JOCKEY PACKAGE 1

	Company #1	Company #2
DISC JOCKEY Package 1:		
Number of dedicated power circuits required?		
Venue restrictions/ surcharges for using smoke/fog/haze/dry ice machine, or surcharge for power?		
Area required to setup (L x W):		
Other considerations:		
Cost of Package 1:	$	$
Additional expenses (e.g. meal, gas, mileage):		

Notes:

_____

_____

_____

_____

_____

DISC JOCKEY PACKAGE 2

	Company #1	Company #2
DISC JOCKEY Package 2:		
Number of dedicated power circuits required?		
Venue restrictions/ surcharges for using smoke/fog/haze/dry ice machine, or surcharge for power?		
Area required to setup (L x W):		
Other considerations:		
Cost of Package 2:	$	$
Additional expenses (e.g. meal, gas, mileage):		

Notes:

_____

_____

_____

_____

_____

	Company #1	Company #2
DISC JOCKEY Package 3:		
Number of dedicated power circuits required?		
Venue restrictions/ surcharges for using smoke/fog/haze/dry ice machine, or surcharge for power?		
Area required to setup (L x W):		
Other considerations:		
Cost of Package 3:	$	$
Additional expenses (e.g. meal, gas, mileage):		

Notes:

_____

_____

_____

_____

_____

_____

THE INTERVIEW

After narrowing down the selection of DISC JOCKEYs, the next step is the contract.

The following *ADDENDUM contains "Professional Wedding Disc Jockey" STANDARDS that should either be included WITHIN your disc Jockey & Emcee's written contract, or the standards should be printed out and included with the written contract. While the respective Disc Jockey may not be a member of the CertifyYourDJ.com – Network, the standards should nevertheless be a part of their written contract.

Remember your answer to the question you answered earlier?

What PERCENTAGE does DANCING & ENTERTAINMENT make up, in the overall SUCCESS of your wedding reception?

There can be no doubt that entertainment plays a very important role in the overall success of a wedding reception. Nothing can be left to chance, and to help ensure that noting is, require the Disc Jockey & Emcee to sign off on the standards.

This may be the most special day in your lives! The overall success of any reception may very well **DEPEND** on the *ADDENDUM be signed and included with the LEGALLY BINDING WRITTEN CONTRACT!

Note: CertifyYourDJ.com is the website of the Certify Your Disc Jockey – Network. As a prerequisite to joining the network, Disc Jockeys must agree to uphold the standards and to guarantee them in writing to their wedding clients.

In addition to the standards, it is important to interview prospective Disc Jockeys & Emcees to ensure they have an appropriate demeanor. An experienced Disc Jockey & Emcee can add intimacy and warmth to your reception. A professional Emcee works well with other event professionals, and can successfully guide your reception from start to finish. There is no replacement for a face-to-face interview.

PROFESSIONAL DISC JOCKEY STANDARDS - ADDENDUM

This Addendum forms part of the agreement between _____ (herein DJ) and _____ (herein "Client") dated the _____ day of _____, 20__, herein the Agreement.

WHEREAS the parties hereto agree and accept to the terms set out below;

AND WHEREAS the Client has engaged the DJ to provide DJ services pursuant to an Event as defined in the Agreement;

NOW THEREFORE for $1.00 and other good and valuable consideration the receipt and sufficiency of which is hereby acknowledged the parties hereto agree as follows:

1. DJ shall comply with the following standards set out below in paragraph 1-10 inclusive:
    1. Respond to Client enquiries within agreed upon time frames and in a timely manner;
    2. Use a professional sound system that is suited to the Event;
    3. Bring backup equipment to the event to ensure minimal down time in case of equipment failure (not a call away);
    4. Use music licensed for public performance (i.e. AVLA licensed or record company/ artist compensated) at the event;
    5. Be insured against liability and prove it, when requested by Client;
    6. Have a minimum three years professional wedding DJ and Emcee experience, and be able to prove it to Client's satisfaction;
    7. Maintain a business website with up-to-date contact information;
    8. Fully disclose all expenses. You will not face additional expenses or charges for services other than those clearly defined within the written contract;
    9. Never drink alcohol while at the Event;
    10. The DJ you meet with is the DJ who will perform at the Event.

2. If the DJ does not meet the standards in paragraph 1, 1-10 inclusive above, the full amount of liability to which he or she maybe subject is the amount contracted for services as the DJ regarding the Event.

3. Unless a written notice outlining the terms of any complaint is sent to the DJ within 7 days of the Event the DJ will have been deemed to have fulfilled the terms of this Agreement to the Client's satisfaction and the client thereby is deemed to have certified the DJ having met the standards herein.

4. This Addendum and the Agreement is the entire agreement between the parties with respect to the subject matter contained therein and herein and it shall not be amended except by an instrument in writing signed by all of the parties hereto and shall be binding upon the respective heirs, executors, administrators, assigns and the directors and officers of the parties hereto.

5. The terms of this Addendum are in addition to, not in conflict or derogation of the terms of the Agreement. The terms of this Addendum shall have the same meaning as they have as set out in the Agreement.

6. The parties hereto acknowledge the terms of the Agreement are in full force and effect and shall do commit no act or omission which may breach or cause the breach of the terms of the Agreement.

AGREED TO AND ACKNOWLEDGED BY:

_____   _____
Client Name: DJ:

Per:

WEDDING VENDOR CONTACT LIST

Vendor	Contact Name	Telephone & Cell Phone	Website & Email
Bridal Consultant		Tel: Cell:	Web: Email:
Cake Baker		Tel: Cell:	Web: Email:
Caterer		Tel: Cell:	Web: Email:
Dress Maker		Tel: Cell:	Web: Email:
Florist		Tel: Cell:	Web: Email:
Officiant		Tel: Cell:	Web: Email:
Photographer		Tel: Cell:	Web: Email:
Reception Venue		Tel: Cell:	Web: Email:
Tuxedo Rental		Tel: Cell:	Web: Email:
Videographer		Tel: Cell:	Web: Email:
Wedding Venue		Tel: Cell:	Web: Email:
		Tel: Cell:	Web: Email:
		Tel: Cell:	Web: Email:

COPYRIGHT NOTICE

Professional Disc Jockey Standards – ADDENDUM has been ratified by Entertainment Lawyer, Paul Sanderson.

PAUL SANDERSON: SANDERSONLAW.CA

Exclusively serving clients in arts and entertainment for over 25 years.

- Consistently named "Most Frequently Recommended" as an entertainment lawyer in the Canadian legal directory "LEXPERT" (www.lexpert.ca)
- Listed in the 2007 & 2010 Special Report of "The Best Lawyers in Canada" in the Entertainment Law category under Music.
- Listed in the 2011 edition of "The Best Lawyers In Canada" in the practice area of Entertainment Law.
- The leading writer on legal aspects of Canadian music law and visual arts
- Author and editor of "Musicians and the Law in Canada"
- Co-author of "Artists' Contracts: Agreements for Visual and Media Artists"

*ADDENDUM - LIMITATION OF LIABILITY